Harmonic Hues

An Anthology of Life's Everyday Moments

Sharon Liz Hermon

BookLeaf Publishing

India | USA | UK

Dedication

To my family and to all the readers who are
joining me in this short journey of poems!

Acknowledgement

I thank God for giving me this wonderful opportunity to write an anthology for the world to see. I thank my family, from my loving parents to my brother, his wife and her family and also my little nephew for their unconditional love, prayers and support. I would like to thank all my teachers for their guidance and inspiration.

Last but certainly not the least, I thank BookLeaf Publishing for providing me with a very user-friendly platform to express my views and make my dream of publishing my work come true.

Preface

The taste of every bit of daily life: 'Harmonic Hues' is the ultimate anthology that everyone can relate to. Reading the fine print of life and noticing each and every detail is something that we all must do. Small incidents might mean a lot if we ponder upon it. Let us be encouraged to consider that each day, each thing and each individual has their own unique story.

The cover page in itself, considering all its elements, is a metaphor. It represents the tunes of everyday life; each day is like a song in the playlist of life.

Take a Breath

Breathe the air around you:
What do you feel?
Did you take in the stench of stress;
Or of darkness and Death?
Or did you take in life's happiness,
All just in one breath?

Filled with joy is the air,
If you don't focus on being in despair.
For even as the tear drops to the ground
It seems to make a beautiful sound.
Breathe the air around you:
What do you feel now?

Rain

I am supposed to be studying
But my mind is not in focus: I am just staring;
Staring at the raindrops.

They seem to fall from the heavens unknown
And wash off all that's dull and gloomy.
They seem to fall like the tears of many
Who mourn for that which they've lost forever.

As lightning strikes and thunder sounds
Are what these people are facing
But through the pain;
Through the clouds;
They endure to see the silver lining.

They hear the music of the rain;
They smell the petrichor
And see the raindrops make the puddles shimmer
As they fall to the ground;
And what holds them through
Is they know that at the end
They'll see the magnificent rainbow.

Sometimes: Other times!

Sometimes you want to run around;
Other times you don't want to make a sound.

Sometimes you want to join the others;
Other times you want to be yourself.

Sometimes you think you could move on;
Other times your flashbacks cloud the dawn.

Sometimes you just have to sit at your table
And think about all that you're able;
Then stop for a moment
And think about all
That you could have done the other times:
Instead of lament!

Rest!

"Just a little; a little bit, please?"
Imagine if we had to take rest on lease!
Our bodies would be sore,
Right up to the core
And we'd pray to God
To give us the old days back!

Now, when we have everything,
We don't value it even a little.
Is it that, when we have nothing,
We realise how blessed we are?
Now ponder, I beg you to.
Then have a well-deserved rest!

Experience

I might be unassuming,
Or maybe too young;
But I think it's worth boasting
That so many times I've sung
The song of innocent mirth,
Because of which I know
The sources of happiness and of its dearth,
And the consequences of believing in things
so low.

I tell you, I grow wiser by the day,
And more so by nights,
That as they say
I won't be 'blinded by the lights',
But I will keep performing my role
To the best of my ability
With all my heart, mind and soul
I won't get distracted and will display my
agility.

I am running for myself and not others,
In this race of life,
O, in this race of life.

Happiness

When you see a kid in a candy store,
Or a toddler in a toy shop
I'm sure the child would implore
Until the wish is fulfilled to the full stop.
And when that's done,
The look in the eyes is pricelessly won.

When you see a young person in a branded
shop,
Admiring all the clothes one wished to own;
When the person finally has the pocket
money to buy one desired top
And have the alterations sewn;
And when that's done,
The look in the eyes is pricelessly won.

When you see a middle-aged person in the
office,
Wishing to get a job promotion
To provide more money, for his family, to
suffice
The boss walks in with 'the' declaration
And when that's done,

The look in the eyes is pricelessly won.

When old people try not to get bored,
But have no one to converse with;
The children, who live far away
Finally plan to come, visit and stay
And when they hear of the plan,
The look in the eyes is pricelessly won.

Young Heart, Old Body

Live your life to the fullest
With what you are blest.
'Memento vivere' stands so true:
But it must be understood by you.
No one will realize that
A lot of time has passed by
As soon as you tip your hat;
And soon there won't be time to cry
Because you'll be too old to live
And too young to die:
Your heart will wish to strive
But your body will be too old to soar high.

So do your best to be remembered tomorrow:
When you're gone.

Habits Quotient

One promises oneself
Never to do the same thing again
By leaving that habit on the top shelf
Unreachable to any thought in the brain;
But no matter how far
No matter how tough the terrain is
We still reach out even if in a broken-down
car
To find momentary bliss.

Before going to rest
You thank God for what He's blest
Assuring Him the rest
Promising that you'll be the best
But the next moment you're back
With the same old slack:
Playing the Music track,
Eating many a snack,
Glued to the phone:
Bent body to the core of the bone;
Being an addict,
Without even knowing it.

Cycle of Life

Everyone says life's a cycle
But no one knows the deep meaning.
I took it this way for instance,
And it sure left me thinking.
Well, money should not be priority
But it is something
That helps us in our daily lives
Without which we would be barely living
In this world with cold hearts and minds
Who only like investing:
Not in lives of individuals in need,
But in stocks, mutual funds and more.
"For what?", you may ask,
To find the answer is a task
For they are not the ones to blame
Since we all are part of creating the desire,
The longing for increasing material wealth
To prove one's status in the world.

Fading Friends

O Friend, when I see you mingling with other
friends of mine
Becoming more closer by the day,
I just feel that one day I will be long forgotten
And your friendship with them will stay.

O Friend, I wish we could all be friends
together,
But no matter how hard we try,
It never seems to work.
Of course you'd be more friendly
With an enemy you've known for years,
Than with a newcomer, a total stranger!

Late

My elder brother and I don't talk much
Since we have a huge age gap
And because of the different phases of life
That each of us are living.

But one day, he approached me
As if to say something important:
And he said something
That I had never thought even once.

It was deep and meaningful;
A little bit scary
If you kept thinking about it,
But it's worth knowing.

"It is better late than never", he said
And with a flourish of his hand,
He asked me if I knew the meaning
Of this saintly, ancient proverb.

I said, "Well, yes of course I do!"
And to that he said
That he bet I never will discover

His newfound interpretation of it.

Well, I didn't know
What he was talking about;
But I sure did know the proverb meant that
Doing something late is better than not doing
it at all.

Then with another flourish of his hand
He presented to me his version:
"I'm sure you didn't think about this", he said;
I was left in suspense for a little longer

"Well, what if someone is late to complete an
assignment,
It is better for him to complete it late,
Because none of us know his fate,
Whether he will never be able to do it if he is
gone tomorrow."

It is never too late until it is.

Ad libitum

When you dive deep into thought,
And think of things of all sort,
I must tell you that you ought
To jot down the experience brought
Into your head as imaginations fought
To make you a lesson taught:
That is, to express your feelings ad libitum!

The Urge

The urge to do the opposite
Is a very real feeling!

This is what I mean to say
And I know everyone has this urge come what
may
And I know you all can relate.

When you see an opportunity:
And just before others see; you reach out your
hand,
An elder instructs to do the same thing,
Just as you planned,
Then the urge; the urge to do the opposite
sets in!

Letting Go

Out of many, many a sorrow
In this world so shallow,
The most pain of all
Is letting go.

Letting go of something
Which will be handed to another.
Letting go of people,
So that in life you can go further.
Letting go of loved ones
As they leave you for a better place forever.

Unspoken Words

There might be someone;
Someone you used to know
Who left you or whom you left
Supposing you can move on;
And you did too:
But one too many times,
Memories come alive,
And you wish you could go back;
Go back in time,
Just to say some unspoken words.

There might be someone;
A very close loved one
Who left the earth for the heavenly abode;
And supposing you could move on;
And you somehow did too:
You try hard to stop
Memories from coming alive,
And you wish you just could go back;
Go back in time just once,
Only to say
Some 'Unspoken Words'.

Weight of Choices

The choices that you make
Are not a piece of cake
That it - so lightly you take.
So for your knowledge's sake
I'll try to help you put the brake
To the hasty choices that you make;
Choosing somethings so fake
That you drown even in a lake;
You must get yourself a rake
To help you smoothen your way to awake
To the reality of consequences.

Symphony of everyday

Everyday is a new beginning
And a new opportunity
For a fresh start.
Letting go of the past and moving on
To the future is the only way to keep
progressing

Every day has it's own individual uniqueness:
Like the melody of the birds chirping outside,
Or the pitter-patter of the rain,
Or the smell of burnt soil,
Or the petrichor of abundant showers.
Neither the bright sun can be compared
To the colourful rainbow after a storm
Nor can we compare it otherwise.

Every day is one step closer
To your success;
Either work towards it
Or walk away from it.

Every day is an encouragement to change our
perspective

And look at life more positively
And live a happy life.

Every day is a reminder that we have only one
life to live:
Let's make the most of it
For others to be inspired,
And to leave an impact on this world when
we are gone.

Reflections in the Mirror

You tell yourself:
"I'm not worth it",
"I'm not enough";
Well yes, that's true if that's what you believe.

But if you stop listening
To what others have to say about you,
And start listening to what God says about
you:

I am sure that
You will stop depending on people's eyes,
And start looking in the mirror twice
Before you have an opinion about yourself!

You have been crafted beautifully by the hand
of the creator:
And nothing can hide that true fact
If you believe that!

The Passage of Time

Before you know it:
Time passes by;
As at your table you sit,
Or in the blink of an eye,
One could fall in a pit
Or rise so high;
One could quit
Or start to try;
But you have the liberty
To do whatever you want
In the passage of time.

Silent Struggles of Others

We may be having a nice day
But that doesn't mean that everyone's on the same
page:
Some might be struggling;
Some may be grieving

Or we may be having a day of sorrow
But that doesn't mean that everyone's on the same
page:
Some may be having a great day;
A day worth celebrating

You can't let your happiness or sorrow
Be an obstruction to the expression of others'
feelings,
Nor can you let others' celebration, mirth and
song
Or someone's tears
Change the perspective of how you see the day.

The only way to deal with people and situations
like these
Is to empathise not sympathise.

Moments of Clarity

Some days we have instant moments
In which we want to act fast,
As deep in our hearts we know the solution,
And we want to do something
Before the enthusiastic spirit of clarity turns cold.

Sometimes these moments
Come in times unexpected;
Sometimes these moments
Come in times when we are instructed;
Sometimes these moments
Come in times when AI comes to the rescue!
All the same we always cherish these moments.

Imagine a doctor who finally finds a cure
To a disease so rare,
Or a programmer who finally debugs the code,
Or any other professional
Who figures out a solution to a problem,
Or for that matter:
Even a teacher who finally understands the
student,
And the student who understands a concept;
Indeed, we always cherish these moments.